Our
Mysterious
Universe

By Laura Langston

Series Literacy Consultant
Dr Ros Fisher

Pearson Education Limited
Edinburgh Gate
Harlow
Essex CM20 2JE
England

www.longman.co.uk

ISBN 0 582 84153 4

Colour reproduction by Colourscan, Singapore
Printed and bound in China by Leo Paper Products Ltd.

The Publisher's policy is to use paper manufactured from sustainable forests.

The following people from **DK** have
contributed to the development of this product:

Art Director Rachael Foster

Martin Wilson **Managing Art Editor** | **Managing Editor** Marie Greenwood
Peter Radcliffe **Design** | **Editorial** Steve Setford, Selina Wood
Marie Ortu **Picture Research** | **Production** Rosalind Holmes
Richard Czapnik, Andy Smith **Cover Design** | **DTP** David McDonald
Consultant Carole Stott

Dorling Kindersley would like to thank: Rose Horridge, Hayley Smith and Gemma Woodward in
the DK Picture Library; Liz Tyndall for editorial assistance; Johnny Pau for additional cover design work.

Picture Credits: CERN: 28cl; Corbis: Sarah Jackson/Edifice 7tr; DK Images: National Maritime Museum 5cr, 8tl; Galaxy Picture Library: boarders,
pages 1-40, David Cortner 4, Isaac Newton Group 25, Jay Gallaghar/WIYN/NOAO/NSF 18t, Michael Stecker 20, Nigel Sharp/NOAO 1, 16,
Richard Wainscoat 6, STScI 26, 29t; NASA: 21t, 22b, 35t, GSCF/Gemini Observatory/APOD corners P4-40, JPL 11tr, 36t; Science Photo Library:
14tr, 27, 36b, Calvin Larsen 13br, Celestial Image Co. 24b, 24t, 40br, David Mclean 13tr, Dr. Seth Shostak 33, Frank Zullo 37,
John Thomas 12, Tony & Daphne Hallas 3, Tony Hallas 22t; Richard Wainscott: 15bl. Jacket: NASA: (back);
Science Photo Library:/David Parker (front b), /National Optical Astronomy Observatories (front t).

All other images: DK Dorling Kindersley © 2004. For further information see www.dkimages.com
Dorling Kindersley Ltd., 80 Strand, London WC2R ORL

Contents

Our Mysterious Universe

For thousands of years, people have watched the night sky. From groups of stars, or constellations, they have formed pictures of animals, objects, gods and ancient heroes. They have observed the paths that stars follow in regular cycles. They've used these movements of the stars to find directions, to tell time and to plan for planting, harvesting and flood seasons. They have tried to explain unpredictable events, such as streaks of light across the sky. They have asked:

- What are we looking at?
- How can we explain the movements of the stars?
- Where did these celestial bodies come from, and where are they going?

The night sky has been a source of wonder and mystery to observers for thousands of years.

Throughout the ages, people have used their skills and have made tools to help them answer questions about the night sky. Today, our understanding of the **universe** is based on knowledge accumulated from data collected using technologically advanced tools and from astronomers' use of the scientific process.

The Scientific Process

Scientists use the scientific process to discover laws or patterns in the universe.
First, they ask questions and make observations. Then they develop a hypothesis, or possible answer to their questions.
They test their hypotheses with experiments. Finally, they use the data from experiments to develop a theory, which is a likely explanation of their observations.

Astrolabes were first used by astronomers and navigators in the 600s to measure the positions of the Sun, stars and planets.

The telescope was first used to study the sky in 1609. Telescopes gave astronomers larger views of celestial objects and revealed far more detail.

Much of what we know about planets and stars began with observations of how things work on Earth. In the past the regularity of the seasons was used to support theories about the way the Sun revolved around Earth. We have begun to understand more about the vast reaches of space and the smallest particles of matter. Yet we find that the universe may follow laws that we can't explain using our common sense. Every day, we continue to use our intelligence, new tools and the scientific process to explore our mysterious **universe**.

The twin Keck telescopes are located on the summit of Mauna Kea in Hawaii, United States, high above the cloud and water vapour of the lower atmosphere.

The Solar System

In ancient times, people explained the universe by what they saw in the sky. The movement of the Sun, the Moon, planets and stars, for example, made Earth appear to be at the centre of the universe. There was a problem, however. Not all of the planets moved smoothly across the sky. Some appeared to reverse direction now and then. How could this be?

Stonehenge in England was used as an astronomical calendar. Its huge stones aligned with the Sun.

Ptolemy's Universe

Ancient Greek astronomers worked hard to understand this mystery. Their work was used by Claudius Ptolemy. He was an astronomer, mathematician and geographer who lived in Egypt during the second century. Ptolemy studied heavenly bodies. He even wrote a catalogue of 1,025 stars that is the basis of today's modern star catalogues. He used observations and mathematics to "prove" that the Earth did not move. Rather, it sat at the centre of everything. This Ptolemaic system was accepted in Europe as fact for about 1,400 years.

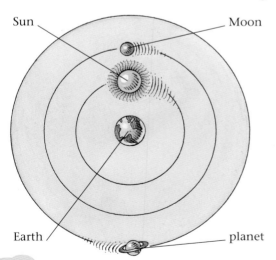

According to Ptolemy, the Sun, the Moon, planets and stars all rotated around the Earth.

7

Revolutionary Ideas

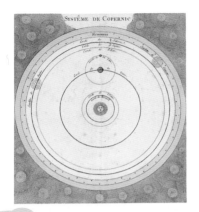

This seventeenth-century illustration shows a plan of the solar system with the Sun at the centre.

The Renaissance brought changes to the ideas about the movement of the stars and planets. In 1543, the Polish scientist Nicolaus Copernicus (1473–1543) suggested that the Sun, not the Earth, was at the centre of the **universe**. This idea was very disturbing to many people.

Other scientists made observations that supported Copernicus's hypothesis. Using a telescope, the Italian scientist Galileo Galilei (1564–1642) saw that the movements of Venus could mean only one thing – that Venus orbits the Sun. Later, the German astronomer Johannes Kepler (1571–1630) discovered that all planets follow oval-shaped paths around the Sun. As a result of their work, they suggested that the six known planets – Mercury, Venus, Earth, Mars, Jupiter and Saturn – orbited around the Sun. Astronomers today know there are more than six planets. Uranus was discovered in 1781 and Neptune's existence was confirmed in 1846.

The Nebular Hypothesis

1. The solar system started as a massive spinning cloud of gas and dust.

2. Gravity caused the Sun to form, and the cloud settled into a disk.

3. Planetesimals formed in the disk.

Formation of the Solar System

Astronomers have developed a theory to explain how the Sun and planets formed.

According to the **nebular hypothesis**, the Sun formed about 5 billion years ago in the hot, dense centre of a spinning cloud of gas and dust. Around that centre, gravity pulled together tiny particles of gas, dust and rock into grain-sized lumps. Slowly these lumps, called **planetesimals**, joined together to form planets. The planets all travelled in the same direction around the Sun at different speeds and at different distances. They were all held in place by the Sun's strong gravity. Gravity played a large role in the formation of our solar system and universe.

Viking probe

Robotic space probes have visited the planets and many of their moons.

The Force of Gravity

All objects are attracted to each other by the force of gravity. More massive objects, such as the Sun, attract more strongly than less massive objects, such as the planets. The closer two objects are to each other, the stronger the pull of gravity will be between them. Sir Isaac Newton (1642–1727) was the first to recognize that gravity explains why objects fall, as well as why objects (such as the Moon) are held in orbit around other objects (such as the Earth).

4. Planetesimals joined together to form planets.

Planetary Bodies

The four planets closest to the Sun – Mercury, Venus, Earth and Mars – are called inner or **terrestrial planets**. They are made of rock. They are also smaller than the outer **Jovian planets** – Jupiter, Saturn, Uranus and Neptune – which are mostly made of gas. These huge outer planets are also called gas giants.

The inner and outer planets are separated by the asteroid belt, a band of many millions of smaller objects called **asteroids** (or minor planets) that orbit the Sun. These asteroids can be between tens of metres wide and several hundred kilometres wide.

An Alternative Theory

A few scientists disagree with the **nebular hypothesis**. They think the planets formed when a cloud of gas and dust passed close to the young Sun and lost some of its material to the Sun's gravitational pull. For years, the only way to test these theories was to use information gathered from looking at our solar system. Recently, however, astronomers have found other stars with orbiting planets. These discoveries may help us learn more about the beginnings of our own solar system.

The Solar System

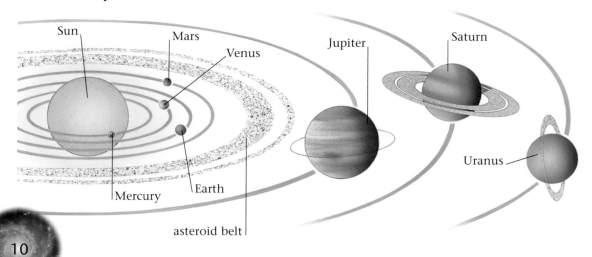

Sun | Mars | Venus | Jupiter | Saturn

Mercury | Earth | Uranus

asteroid belt

10

The Puzzle of Pluto

Scientists believe that Pluto is a small, cold ball of rock and ice. When it was discovered in 1930, it was the ninth planet from the Sun. Then, in 1979, something extraordinary happened. Its orbit took it closer to the Sun than Neptune. In 1999, it crossed back into ninth place. Scientists now realize that, because of the shape of Pluto's orbit, for 20 years during each of Pluto's 248-year orbits, Neptune is actually the furthest planet from the Sun.

This picture of Pluto (left) and its moon Charon (right) was taken by the Hubble Space Telescope.

Pluto has other peculiarities. Its moon, Charon, is half as big as Pluto. None of the other planets has such a relatively large moon. As a result of these discoveries, many scientists believe that Pluto is a minor planet, like an asteroid.

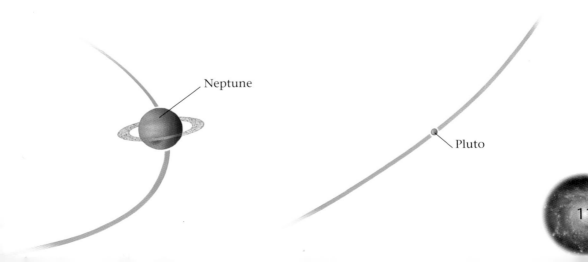

Neptune

Pluto

Visible from Earth in 1996, Comet Hyakutake had one of the longest tails observed in the last fifty years.

Comets – Occasional Visitors

Comets are balls of snow, ice and dust that have changed only slightly since the Sun and planets were formed. Some orbit the Sun in the Kuiper belt, beyond Neptune. Most are even farther away, at the edge of the solar system, in a region known as the Oort cloud.

Now and then, a comet is pulled by a passing star into an orbit that takes it near the Sun. The solar heat quickly turns some of the comet's snow to a gas. The comet's glowing head has two long tails of gases and dust that are pushed away from the comet by the Sun. The glowing head and tails make a comet visible from Earth.

Shooting Stars and Meteorites

Meteors, or "shooting stars", are sudden streaks of light across the sky. They are the result of dust or debris from a comet or **asteroid** that burns up as it passes through the Earth's atmosphere. When a piece of rocky debris is too big to burn up and plunges through the atmosphere to reach Earth it is called a **meteorite**. Scientists study meteorites to determine the age and type of material found in other parts of the solar system.

Meteors in a shower seem to come from a specific area in the sky, called the shower's radiant.

Meteorites range in size from almost invisible dust particles to massive boulders. Although meteorites may help us answer some questions about our solar system, they often lead to more questions.

For example, could huge meteorites falling on Earth have led to animal extinctions? Many astronomers think that the dinosaurs died out when a 9-kilometre-wide meteorite hit Central America 65 million years ago and changed the Earth's climate. Scientists in different fields are testing these theories.

This huge crater in Arizona, United States, called Barringer Crater, was formed about 50,000 years ago when a meteorite about 30 metres wide struck the Earth.

Star Facts

Of all the stars, we know the Sun best because it is the closest star to Earth. Thousands of years ago, people recognized that the Sun made life on the Earth possible. Galileo was one of the first who studied the Sun in detail. Using his telescope, he observed **sunspots**, or dark patches on the Sun's surface, at the beginning of the 17th century.

Sunspots were the first sign that the Sun is not a uniform ball of fire.

Since Galileo's time, more information has been gathered about the Sun, using such tools as powerful telescopes, spectrographs (devices that break down light into the colours of the spectrum) and electronic cameras. We now know that energy travels outwards from the Sun's core and leaves the surface, or photosphere, on its way into space.

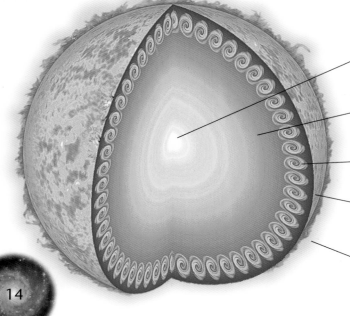

Layers of the Sun

Nuclear reactions produce energy in the core.

Energy travels through the radiative zone as tiny particles called **photons**.

In the convective zone, energy is carried by currents of hot gas.

The Sun's visible surface is called the photosphere.

Beyond the photosphere is the chromosphere, the first layer of the Sun's atmosphere.

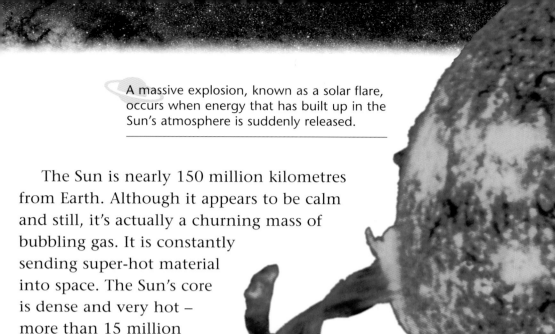

A massive explosion, known as a solar flare, occurs when energy that has built up in the Sun's atmosphere is suddenly released.

The Sun is nearly 150 million kilometres from Earth. Although it appears to be calm and still, it's actually a churning mass of bubbling gas. It is constantly sending super-hot material into space. The Sun's core is dense and very hot – more than 15 million degrees Kelvin (about 16 million degrees Celsius). It releases tremendous amounts of energy.

This energy takes thousands of years to reach the Sun's surface. Then that energy is released. Some of it reaches Earth eight minutes later as sunlight.

The outer part of the solar atmosphere is the corona. It can be seen as a milky white crown when the Moon passes in front of the Sun during a total solar eclipse.

The Life Cycle of Stars

The Sun isn't the biggest star or the oldest. Studying the Sun has helped us learn about other stars. By watching different stars at different stages in their development, we learn how they form and how they change over time. Stars form in a **nebula**, a giant cloud of gas and dust. Over millions of years, the gas and dust come together in clumps called **protostars**. Gravity pulls the gas and dust together making it more densely packed. Once the core of a protostar becomes hot and dense enough, the star shines.

Astronomers observe nebulae to learn about star formation. Shown here is the Horsehead Nebula, in the constellation of Orion.

The Life of a Star

1. A star like the Sun shines for billions of years during its main sequence lifetime.

2. At the end of its main sequence lifetime, the star swells into a red giant.

3. Outer layers are blown away, and the core, a white dwarf, cools and eventually becomes dark.

The **mass** of a star – the amount of matter it contains – determines its future. The greater the mass, the brighter and hotter the star will be. Massive stars, however, burn up more quickly than smaller ones.

When a star the size of our Sun gets very old, its core begins to collapse under the force of gravity. As it collapses, the core heats up drastically. The star swells, sometimes to more than 100 times its original size. Once the star's surface is cooled, it is called a **red giant**. Eventually the star's outer shell blows away and creates a cloud of dust and gas. The remaining core is very hot and dense and is called a **white dwarf**. The white dwarf will eventually cool and become dark.

How Heavy Are the Stars?

The mass of a star is usually measured in relation to our Sun. The mass of our Sun is about 333,000 times that of Earth. Stars can be from 1/10 the mass of our Sun up to as heavy as 100 Suns.

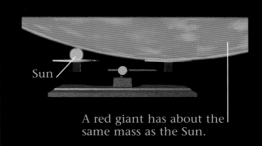

Sun

A red giant has about the same mass as the Sun.

A star more than eight times the **mass** of our Sun doesn't end as a **red giant**. Its core is so dense and hot that it can produce still more energy. When the massive star finally collapses, its core forms a very dense **neutron star**. Its outer layers explode into space, producing a **supernova** that shines brilliantly for a short time and then fades away.

The Crab **Nebula** is the remnant of a supernova explosion seen in 1054. At the centre of the nebula there is a neutron star.

The dust and gases thrown into space by a supernova can form new stars (and planetary systems). Our Sun, the planets in the solar system, and all living things on Earth come from the remnants of at least one supernova. So, we could say that our planet is made of stardust.

The Death of a Massive Star

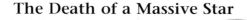

neutron star

black hole

1. A star about eight or more times the mass of the Sun shines for millions of years.

2. Near the end of its life, it swells into a red supergiant.

3. When this star collapses, it explodes as a supernova.

4. The core then forms a neutron star or perhaps a **black hole**.

A Black Hole's Effect on a Nearby Star

A swirling disk of gas surrounds the black hole.

Hot gas gives off X-rays (wavy lines on diagram) as it is drawn into the black hole.

Streams of gas are pulled off a nearby star by the black hole.

Locating Black Holes

Since no light can escape a black hole, nobody has ever observed one. Scientists can, however, deduce the existence of black holes and observe the effects on their surroundings.

Sometimes astronomers can see a star moving along an orbit but can't see the object it is orbiting. That object may be a black hole.

A black hole may create mirages. When a black hole passes in front of a star, gravity from the black hole bends the light coming from the star. To a viewer watching the star through a telescope, the star then seems brighter than it really is. The black hole's gravity can also make one background star look like two.

A supernova leaves an extremely dense neutron star that spins very fast and sends out pulses of radiation. When we detect the pulses we call it a **pulsar**. Sometimes, however, a supernova does not leave behind a neutron star. Instead it produces an object so dense that not even light can escape its gravity. This object is called a black hole.

Black holes can't be seen, but their effects on nearby stars can be observed. If a black hole is near another star, for example, its gravity can pull the glowing gases from the star into the hole.

Double Stars and Clusters

Our Sun is a middle-aged star. Scientists believe it will last another 5 billion years or so before it begins to expand into a **red giant**. Our Sun is also a solitary star. Many stars, however, have a companion. These pairs are called double stars.

Stars are not evenly spread throughout space. They are often observed in groups, or clusters. Some clusters are loose groups of a few dozen to a few thousand stars. Over time, these clusters break up as the stars drift apart. Other clusters are bigger and brighter. They may contain more than a million stars. Because they are among the oldest objects known, astronomers study them to help determine the age of the **universe**.

The Pleiades is a well-known cluster. It contains about 100 stars.

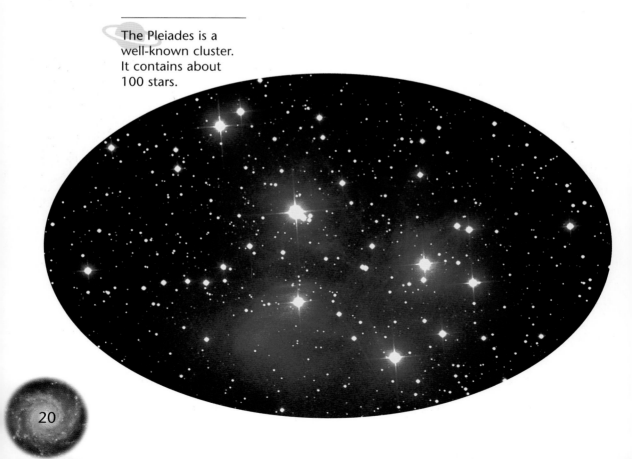

The globular cluster M80 contains hundreds of thousands of stars. It is 28,000 **light-years** from Earth.

Even though stars are far away, astronomers know lots about them. A star's colour and brightness can help show its temperature and size.

Astronomers classify stars into seven types, according to their colour. Blue stars are the hottest, followed by white. Cooler stars look yellow, orange and red.

Measuring Space

What units are used to measure the vast distances of space? One measure is the astronomical unit (a.u.). One a.u. is the distance from the Sun to Earth, or approximately 150 million kilometres. Another unit of measure is the light-year. One light-year is the distance light can travel in one year. Light travels about 300,000 km per second, so one light-year is about 9,460,000,000,000 km.

Types of Stars

The Sun is a Type G star.

TYPE O (40,000–30,500°C)	TYPE B (30,500–9,700°C)	TYPE A (9,700–7,200°C)	TYPE F (7,200–5,800°C)	TYPE G (5,800–4,700°C)	TYPE K (4,700–3,300°C)	TYPE M (3,300–2,200°C)

Galaxies

The Andromeda Galaxy is the furthest point in the universe visible to the unaided human eye.

Hubble Space Telescope

Named after the American astronomer Edwin Hubble (1889–1953), the Hubble Space Telescope was launched in 1990. It orbits the Earth and photographs objects, including those near the edge of the visible universe, such as distant galaxies containing billions of stars.

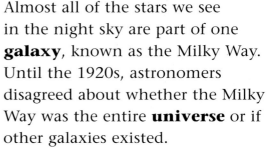

Almost all of the stars we see in the night sky are part of one **galaxy**, known as the Milky Way. Until the 1920s, astronomers disagreed about whether the Milky Way was the entire **universe** or if other galaxies existed.

Edwin Hubble used the most powerful telescope of his time to gather data about the Andromeda **Nebula**. He discovered it was too far away to be part of the Milky Way. This meant that the universe extended beyond our galaxy. Within a few years, astronomers recognized that the universe was made up of many galaxies, including the Andromeda Galaxy.

elliptical galaxy

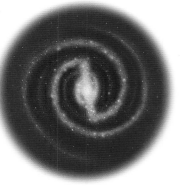

spiral galaxy

barred-spiral galaxy

Gravity holds each
galaxy together, but the
shape of a galaxy
depends on how fast it
spins and how many
new stars are in it.

Categorizing Galaxies

A galaxy is an enormous collection of
stars, dust, gases and planets. Scientists
categorize galaxies by shape: elliptical,
spiral, barred-spiral and irregular.

Elliptical galaxies are oval-shaped like
an egg. These galaxies can be large or
small. They contain old, red stars and a
little dust and gas. Spiral galaxies, like our
own Milky Way, are shaped like disks.
Spiral galaxies bulge in the middle and
have shining spiral arms. They contain
plenty of gases to form new stars.

Barred-spiral galaxies are like spiral
galaxies, but they have a straight bar of
stars across the middle with arms curling
out of each end. New stars are born in the
bars of these galaxies.

Irregular galaxies have no set shape
and are rich in gas and dust. They are
usually the smallest galaxies, with many
young stars and bright gas clouds where
new stars are forming.

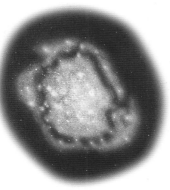

irregular galaxy

The peanut-shaped Small Magellanic Cloud contains about 2,000 star clusters.

Two **galaxies** near the Milky Way, the Large Magellanic Cloud and the Small Magellanic Cloud, are irregular galaxies. They orbit the Milky Way, taking more than a billion years to travel once around it. Gravity holds these two galaxies in place, but it is also working to pull apart the Small Magellanic Cloud. Eventually, the smaller galaxy's stars will probably be pulled into our own Milky Way.

Groups of Galaxies

Gravity keeps galaxies together in groups or clusters. These clusters also form bigger groups called superclusters. Astronomers have identified more than fifty superclusters. Each one contains thousands of galaxies. It would take a beam of light tens of millions of years to cross a supercluster.

The Virgo Cluster is 50 million **light-years** away and contains more than 2,000 galaxies.

The Milky Way, the Andromeda Galaxy and a few smaller galaxies, including the Magellanic Clouds, form the Local Group. How close together are the members of our Local Group? The Andromeda Galaxy is about 2.25 million light-years from the Milky Way. The Magellanic Clouds are much closer – just about 200,000 light-years away.

The irregular galaxy NGC 6822 is one of the galaxies that make up the Local Group. It is 1.75 million light-years away.

Galactic Surprises

Scientists use many different tools – including radio and infrared telescopes – to explore the Milky Way. Near the centre of our **galaxy**, scientists have found very high temperatures and movement of stars. These discoveries have led astronomers to believe there must be a **black hole** in the core of the Milky Way that is 2.5 million times bigger than the Sun.

Some distant galaxies, called **active galaxies**, also seem to give off more energy than expected. The most powerful kind of active galaxy is called a **quasar**. Quasars seem to be quite small and far away but they produce huge amounts of energy. Scientists now believe that they are the cores of galaxies many billions of **light-years** from Earth. The cores may have giant black holes.

Quasars are among the most distant and most powerful objects in the **universe**.

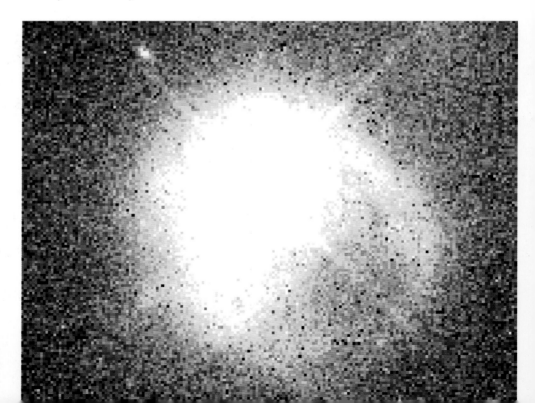

The Big Bang and Other Mysteries

When astronomers developed ways to measure how far galaxies are from Earth, they discovered the stars being observed were moving farther away from our own galaxy. In other words, the universe was expanding, or getting bigger.

Hubble spent years observing distant galaxies and collecting data about how quickly they were moving away. He plotted a graph that showed how fast the universe is expanding. He was able to estimate how long ago all matter in space was in a single spot. That is, the point when it all began. Today, we know that the universe began more than 13 billion years ago.

Edwin Hubble (1889–1953)

How the Universe Began

We do not know exactly what happened at the moment the universe was created. The **Big Bang** theory says that everything in the **universe** was created from a tiny fireball that exploded and began expanding rapidly. For hundreds of thousands of years, the fireball was too hot for matter to exist in the form of atoms. As the universe expanded and cooled, matter eventually formed. This matter was not spread evenly throughout the universe. There were slightly denser patches here and there. These patches would eventually form the **galaxies**, stars, solar systems and planets.

Minute particles, like those created in the hot, dense and hectic conditions of the young universe, can be studied in instruments called particle accelerators.

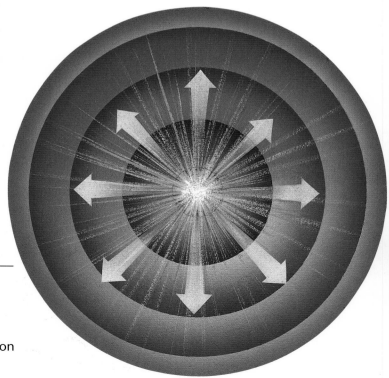

In a fraction of a second after the Big Bang, the universe expanded in size a hundred trillion trillion trillion trillion times.

This picture, taken by the Hubble Space Telescope, shows some of the most distant objects we can see at this time. Some of them are more than 12 billion **light-years** away.

Evidence for the Big Bang

Most astronomers believe the Big Bang best explains how the universe began. They continue to discover data to support the theory. They use tools, such as the Hubble Space Telescope, as time machines to look at galaxies and other objects 12 billion years old or older. Using temperature-detecting radio telescopes and satellites, scientists have discovered a faint and constant hiss spread throughout the universe. They believe the hiss is what is left from the heat of the Big Bang.

This satellite image, made in 1992, shows differences in temperature which gives clues about how galaxies were formed.

The red patches show where radiation is most dense.

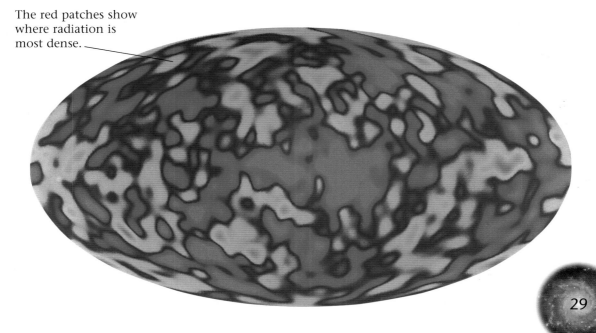

The Fate of the Universe

Today, astronomers are trying to work out what will happen to the **universe**. If it continues to expand forever, the **galaxies** will drift further apart. The stars in the galaxies will eventually die. Even the **black holes** will cease to exist. This is called the open universe theory.

If there is enough **mass** in the universe, gravity will stop it from expanding. The universe will then collapse in on itself in a Big Crunch. All matter will come together into a single point. The end of our universe might also be the start of a new universe – one that could follow entirely different laws of nature from those we currently experience. This is called the closed universe theory.

Open Universe

3. Supermassive black holes disappear, leaving only **white dwarves** and **neutron stars**.

2. Supermassive black holes form in centres of dying galaxies.

Closed Universe

3. Each galaxy is now a supermassive black hole surrounded by the remains of stars. The universe gets smaller and the galaxies move closer together.

2. The stars and galaxies begin to die. The universe stops expanding.

1. Galaxies use up their gas and dust. No new stars form.

4. White dwarves and neutron stars collapse, forming new black holes that soon disappear.

5. The expanding universe becomes cold.

Astronomers are trying to measure the mass of the universe to find out how it will end. All the visible objects – galaxies, stars, gas, dust and planets – don't contain enough mass (with enough gravitational pull) to collapse the universe. What we see in space is only part of what is actually there. Scientists have discovered that most of the matter in the universe is **dark matter** – material that doesn't give off any light. Astronomers know dark matter exists because its gravity pulls on stars and other visible matter.

4. The remains of the stars boil away into space as the background temperature increases. Galaxies merge.

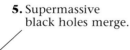

5. Supermassive black holes merge.

6. Universe disappears into a single mega black hole – the Big Crunch.

Missing Matter

The missing dark matter may come in several forms. One possibility is something called a MACHO (Massive Compact Halo Object). MACHOs include dim brown dwarf stars and, possibly, tiny black holes. Another possibility could be a WIMP (Weakly Interacting Massive Particle). Some scientists suspect WIMPs exist everywhere and could make up 90 per cent of the matter in the universe. These scientists are working on developing equipment and experiments to detect WIMPs.

Is Anybody Out There?

Scientists are also researching whether life exists in places other than the Earth. At the moment, Earth is the only known place in the **universe** with life. However, the elements needed for life – carbon, hydrogen and oxygen – are common in space. Sun-like stars with planets revolving around them have been discovered in the Milky Way. Billions of **galaxies** are also in the universe, each of which could contain stars with solar systems. Could there be any intelligent life in these galaxies?

Different conditions on other planets might produce creatures like this artist's idea.

The world's largest single-dish radio telescope, the Arecibo dish, is built into a natural hollow in the hills of Puerto Rico.

Scientists are looking into the possibility of life on other planets. Radio telescopes are used to listen for signs of life and to send signals from Earth into space. Some are used to study radiation from stars and **nebulae**.

South of Arecibo, Puerto Rico, is a huge radio telescope more than 300 metres wide. Scientists come from all over the world to use the telescope. In 1974, some of them sent a message into outer space using the telescope's radio transmitters. The message was aimed at a cluster of stars. It will take 23,000 years for the message to reach its destination. If there is ever a reply, it will take that long for a message to come back.

Looking Closer to Home

Obviously, distances in space make the search for extra-terrestrial life challenging. In today's spacecraft it would take tens of thousands of years for people to travel from Earth to Alpha Centauri, the nearest star to the Sun. It takes 4.3 years for a message travelling at the speed of light to reach there from the Earth.

Scientists are also looking for life within our own solar system. Some of the planets can be ruled out. Mercury and Venus are probably too hot. Uranus and Neptune are probably too cold. However, scientists wonder about Mars.

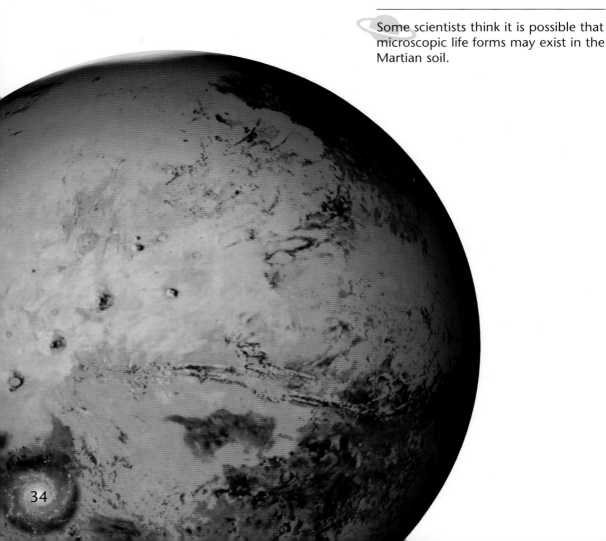

Some scientists think it is possible that microscopic life forms may exist in the Martian soil.

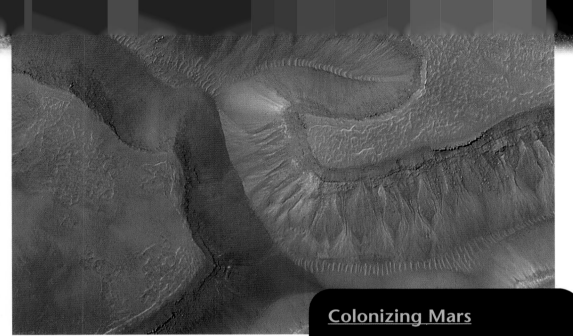

The Viking space probe photographed long Martian channels that may once have held running water.

Space probes began exploring Mars in the 1960s. Since then, more robotic spacecraft have followed. They have collected soil samples and taken pictures. From these, we have learned that Mars once had water on its surface and an atmosphere. We know it has volcanoes larger than anything on Earth and ice caps at both of its poles. Scientists continue to study its soil. They also study **meteorites** believed to be from Mars that fell to Earth thousands of years ago.

Colonizing Mars

Perhaps someday we could change the environment on Mars so that life from Earth could survive there. It might take centuries, but if we could find a way of releasing the carbon dioxide that is trapped in the Martian surface, plants would be able to grow and eventually an oxygen atmosphere would develop on Mars.

Mars

Giant mirrors orbiting Mars might someday be used to melt carbon dioxide trapped in the Martian ice caps and rocks.

sunlight

orbiting mirror

The moons of Saturn and Jupiter also interest astronomers. Titan, Saturn's largest moon, has an atmosphere similar to Earth's. The Galileo space probe has sent back pictures of Europa, one of Jupiter's moons, showing massive ice floes, or sheets of ice. Scientists wonder if a huge ocean exists beneath the floes.

These moons are so far away from the Sun that they should be too cold for life. Volcanic activity or the gravitational influence of Jupiter, however, could make them warm enough to support living things.

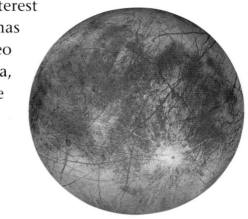

It is possible that simple aquatic life may exist on Europa if there are oceans under its frozen surface.

Space probes, as shown here in this artist's rendering, will help scientists to discover whether Titan could support life.

What Next?

Over the centuries, our understanding of the **universe** has increased. Many questions have been answered, but many more have been raised. We can observe distant objects, from incredibly tiny particles to **galaxies** near the edge of the visible universe.

One thousand years ago, many people believed they understood the universe, with the Earth at the centre of everything. Now we believe we have a more accurate picture of the universe, with Earth positioned in one spiral arm of one galaxy in a universe with no centre. What will we discover about our mysterious universe in the next thousand years?

We still have much to discover about the universe.

Glossary

active galaxies   galaxies that send out more energy than expected from starlight alone

asteroids   rocky bodies orbiting the Sun

Big Bang   a theory that the universe started with a huge explosion, creating all matter, space and time

black hole   an area in space with such strong gravity that not even light can escape from it

dark matter   unseen matter that is known to exist because of its pull on other things in space

galaxy   a collection of stars, gas, dust and planets held together by gravity

Jovian planets   Jupiter, Saturn, Uranus and Neptune; also called the outer planets, or gas giants

light-year   a unit of measurement used by astronomers based on the distance light can travel in a year

mass   the amount of matter in an object

meteorite   a piece of rocky debris that lands on Earth

nebula   a huge cloud of gas and dust; plural **nebulae**

nebular hypothesis   a theory that says that the Sun and its planets formed at the centre of a nebula

neutron star   an extremely dense core of a star left after a supernova explosion

planetesimals	rocky objects that combined to form planets
protostars	stars just starting the process of becoming stars
pulsar	a rapidly spinning neutron star
quasar	the core of a galaxy containing a giant black hole that produces a tremendous amount of energy
red giant	a star in the later stages of its life cycle
sunspots	dark spots visible on the Sun's surface caused by disturbances in the Sun's magnetic field
supernova	an exploding star
terrestrial planets	the planets Mercury, Venus, Earth and Mars that are mostly made of rock and metal; also called the inner planets
universe	everything that exists, including the planets, stars, gas, dust, galaxies and space
white dwarf	an old star

Index